Reclaimed Land

A Sixties Childhood

Reclaimed Land

A Sixties Childhood

Graham Fulton

The Grimsay Press

Published by:

The Grimsay Press
An imprint of Zeticula Ltd
The Roan
Kilkerran
KA19 8LS
Scotland
http://www.thegrimsaypress.co.uk

First published in 2013

Text and photographs © Graham Fulton 2013

ISBN 978-1-84530-138-5

for the people inside

Life is a blur. It goes along and it's gone. The moments fuse. Become one. But some times burn bright. Pulse. Sparkle. Above the rest.

Is Graham coming out to play?

Is the 60s coming out to play?

The House. Walking on floorboards. Not finished. Where we are going to be. Soon. It'll be ready soon. Here. This. Walking the floorboards. The walls, the ceilings, the half-born house. Semi-detached. A skeleton waiting for flesh. The stairs up. The stairs down. Keanie the builders. Hammering, sawing. The blank gardens at the front and the back. A beginning waiting to breathe.

The curve of a slowly sloping downwards road. A driveway. A car in the driveway. A registration number. A garage. Everything in place. Nothing amazing. Ours. Our chimney. Our fire. The future is unafraid.

On top of a pyramid of bricks in the middle of the road. Me and Gordon. My older brother. Gloves and duffel coats. Rubble and cement. Cold and grey. They're building more houses. *I'm the king of the castle, you're the dirty wee rascal.* New houses for new people. Us. We're some of the new people. Building paths through empty space.

First winter at 55 Atholl Crescent, Ralston, Paisley. Ralston pronounced Rawlston. Building a snowman in the back garden. No trees yet. No time to grow. Just us and the snow and our spades. The high wall behind us. Pieces of coal for buttons and eyes. The snow sparkling on our hoods and balaclavas. Smiling for the camera. It took weeks to melt. A little bit less every day. One day I looked and it wasn't there. As if it had never existed at all.

At the side of my bed saying my prayers. God bless Mummy and Daddy, and God bless Gordon and Granny Fulton and Granny McLardie. Hands together. Eyes shut. The bump of the hot water bottle under the blankets. A potty on the floor. A medicine glass with a tooth under it.

A lump of sugar being placed on my tongue.   Covered in something to stop me catching something else.

Faint, but there. Definitely there. A funeral on the television in black and white.   Hundreds of walking people.   Horses. Drums beating and a music of death.   The name Kennedy. Everyone sad. The sadness seeps in. The feeling is absorbed. Remains.

The tide was out and we ran to the far away sea with the sun glinting off the sandy ripples. *Look after Graham.* Gordon and me and cousins Anne and Kenneth.   Swimming trunks. The slap of our holiday feet.   Excited. I stopped and turned back.   It was too far. I didn't tell anyone. I wanted to play with my bucket and spade instead.   I couldn't find mum and dad and walked along crying with thousands of people looking at me. Faces. Crying. A deckchair man took me in and put a towel over my shoulders and gave me a cup of tea with midges floating on it. People looking at me. I rode on the handlebars of his big black bicycle to the police station. Tears forgotten.   Mum and dad came in later.   Desperate. Lots of hugging.   Laughing.   What life's all about.

In the middle of the night the water pipes would make a loud thumping noise. We'd wake. It's only air in the pipes. Nothing to be afraid of. *Go back to sleep. It'll stop soon.* Very soon. Like something trying to get inside. Thump. Something trying to escape. Thump. We knew it was there, looking for us.

New flats being built around the corner. We went to look and got stuck in the mud. Couldn't move. A boy we called Chinka-China ran and got mum. She came round and got a plank of wood and went along it and pulled us out. No messing. Straight up. One of a mother's many jobs. Our Wellington boots stayed where they were. Probably found in 2,000 years time. The last trace of a vanished race.

At Uncle Tom and Aunt Nancy's. High tenement windows. One or two floors up. A view of grass outside in the sunshine. Watching My Favourite Martian on the telly, or reading My Favourite Martian in a comic. One or the other. An early memory. Half of it there, half of it mist. Trying to find where it's meant to be.

First day of school. Posing for a photo on the garden steps. Tie. Shirt. Shorts. Socks. Ralston Primary School badge on the cap. The world quickly gets bigger. Somehow smaller.

Dad. Lighting the fire in the early darkness. Twisting pieces of newspaper. Placing the coals. Emptying the dead grey ash. The television sparking to life. The theme tune of the Tokyo Olympics. The flames rising. Dad. Washing the dishes. Driving his car. Tapping away at his typewriter upstairs. Finishing his reports. Getting a better paid job one day and mum hugging him and laughing and everyone really excited. Putting brown paper covers on our school jotters. Polishing our shoes. Dad. Buying a Bang and Olufsen stereo system. Taking us to Crookston Castle. Battleships on the Clyde. Taking us to Kelvingrove to see the fossils in the cases. Taking us to lochs. Water. Hills. Ben Lomond. We could see the top. Too high. We were too tired and had to turn back. Useless. Dad didn't mind. Watching us as we totter insanely on the second floor beams of the new flats being built and telling us to slowly carefully make our way down. Buying us comics and books. Putting a thermometer in our mouths when we got sick. Making sure it was all okay.

Mum starting with the big toe and working her way along. *This little piggy went to market.* Slowly. *And this little piggy went ... wee wee wee all the way home.* Finally the big tickle. Bouncing on mum's crossed leg as she sang *Bumpity! Bumpity! Bumpity! Bump! As if I was riding my charger.* The essence of childhood. Nothing to worry us. Nothing to be responsible for. Nothing but the very second.

Sitting beside the washing contraption. Mum at the mangle. The rollers. The thick soapy heat. Turning the handle. She told me about her dad and how he died when he was very young. How he was once at a place called Gallipoli. She said he talked about the young boys crying for their mothers. He was just a boy himself. Mum was only ten when he died. I don't know if he said this to her face, or if she heard it from somebody else. Sometime later. Bits of the story lost in the steam. The bits in between. In the kitchen, listening. The clothes. Mum.

The car turning down Well Street. Past the gasworks. Round sleeping giants. Past the shop at the corner and into Tannahill Road. The steps and the door at the side and the stairs going up. The view from Granny McLardie's front window. An oval island with trees and a fence around it. A road around the island. Houses around the road. It seemed far away. I was never on the island. The view from gran's kitchen window. A garden shared with the people downstairs. I was never in the garden. I don't think. Bushes at the bottom and something else beyond.

Staying over at gran's house.   Lying in the bed settee.
Comforting mattress.   Blankets up to our necks.   Gran on
her chair in the half dark.   The black and white glow from
the television.   The sound down low so as not to disturb us.
The coal fire.   The strange human figure carved lamp stand.
A bit scary.   He's watching us.   The piano and the red velvet
covered stool.   The treadle of the sewing machine.   A small
pale purple cushion with pins stuck into it.   The things of
daylight have gone elsewhere.   Another dream.   They'll be
back when we wake.

We'd come home from gran's and it's cold and dark.   Dad
would light the fire with paper and coal.   As we waited
mum would wrap her coat around us and hold us inside.
A winter coat.   Cream coloured.   The flames would begin.
The dark was replaced.   We didn't want to leave.   We were
warm.   Safe.   Stayed as long as we could.   All time.   Here.
Like a womb.

Relatives are visiting and the television is on in the
background.   A programme about cinema.   I'm on mum's
knee.   Suddenly the shower scene from Psycho begins.   I
didn't know what it was.   No warning.   A woman screaming.
A silhouette.   The water, the knife, the music.   Especially the
music.   The cruel monochrome music.   I closed my eyes,
buried my face against mum.   The sound went on and on.
The sound of everything bad in the world.   Rhythm, terror.
All mixed up.   Less than a minute.   My favourite film.

I entered a Blue Peter competition.   Draw a monster for Doctor Who.   I was sure to win.   A blob with a huge eye and seven legs.   Mum sent it off.   They showed the winners on the screen and displayed the best of the rest.   A gallery of horror.   The camera slowly panning across.   Mine was nowhere to be seen.

Spinning around on the dining room carpet.   Arms outstretched.   Circling inside the world.   Time and space a blur.   Faster, faster, then suddenly stop.   Standing still but the inside of your head still going.   Fabulous imbalance. Dizzy, wobbling, stumbling, laughing, falling over.   Getting up and doing it again.

Gordon sometimes had nettle rash in the middle of the night. All of a sudden.   No reason.   The way it is.   Thrashing and screaming in pain until mum would soothe it away.   Till the next time.

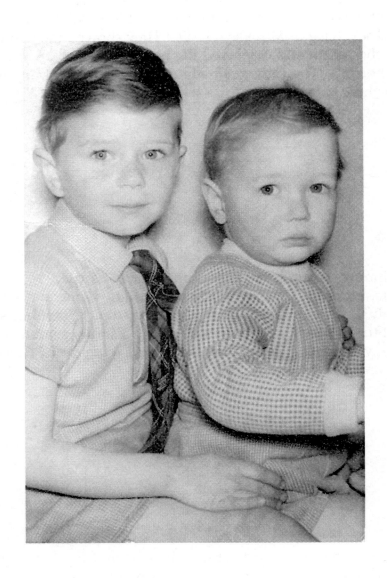

Things on the bedroom walls.   Posters saying Pan Am and BOAC.   Come to Tel Aviv.   Something about Canada with pictures of totem poles and Mounties.   A picture of Jesus and some children in a thin black frame.   *Suffer the little children to come to me.*   A picture of Tommy Steele cut from a magazine.   Spitfires and Messerschmitts hanging from the ceiling.   Things removed.   Replaced.   Covered over. Vanished.   Flower pattern wallpaper later pasted by Thunderbirds.   A big toy box made of some strange material under the bed.   Bullet holes on the windows.

In a quiet cinema with mum. Afternoon matinee. Watching A Hard Day's Night.   The Beatles running about on the grass.   Being silly in Black and White.   The birth of the new. Afterwards to Arnotts tea room with its big windows in the full colour sunshine.   Bread and butter and cakes on a stand. As smart as can be.   Real Paisley posh.

Mum and dad had an LP called San Remo Festival. A green cover with drawings on it.   Volare.   Songs sung in Italian. Some jolly. Some sad. One sounded like the man was singing *Under my Corry,* so that's what we repeated in silly voices. But one or two really got me.   A woman singing.   Io Amo, Tu Ami.   Sweeping violins that ached inside.   Particular chords played in the right order. Music reaching me for the first time. I don't remember her name.

One morning I woke and looked at the clock and it was five minutes to nine and mum and dad were still fast asleep and I went in and shook them awake with a scared look on my face and we all got dressed really fast and didn't have time for anything to eat and ran round to the school and got there for one minute past nine and nobody knew.

I wouldn't eat mince. I didn't like the slimy bits of onion. I'd move them to the side of the plate or wouldn't touch it at all. Mum and dad at the end of their tethers. Everyone would be in the lounge watching television. The sliding doors closed. I'd still be there half an hour later with my arms folded. Looking straight ahead at the wall with the painting by Constable on it. The mince untouched. Big sighs. They'd finally give me something else I'd take. Egg mashed in a cup, except for the stringy white bits. Cocoa in a mug, except for the rippling skin on the top. It looked alive. Fish, except for the bones. Liver, except for the bits of gristle. Everyone was worried I'd grow up as small as Ronnie Corbett. I'd eat my soup until I saw the lady at the bottom of the bowl. If I got a sandwich I didn't like I'd hide it behind the hallstand.

We had apple pie for pudding. A sharp piece of apple stuck in my throat. Jaggy. Not moving. I'm convinced I'm going to die. To die. I'm six years old. Hardly lived. Mum and dad bring me a glass of water. Watching, asking if I'm okay. *It'll go in time.* The bedroom door half open. The light from the landing. Lying in bed waiting to die. I become calm. I'm ready. Gordon crying. I said *It's All Right.* Gordon telling me he hopes I don't die. The light. The landing. The door slightly open. The piece of apple went down later on. I didn't die.

Seaside town. Candy floss and toffee apples. A separate shallow pool next to the promenade. Next to the sea. I'm walking slowly around the perimeter pulling a string attached to a small blue yacht with a white cloth sail. About nine inches long. It glides silently through the grey British holiday resort water. Soundless. Round and round. One more time. Endlessly patient. Sublime repetition. Waiting for nothing to happen.

I climbed a tree which wasn't very high. 6 feet. No more. Just by the big school gates. I was small. I couldn't get down. I froze. I bubbled. Someone ran for dad and he came and reached out. I let myself go. His arms brought me down. I climbed it again in the future. No problem. Not high at all.

All of us lined up for the school photo. Three rows. The girls at the front. A mix in the middle. Boys at the back standing on a line of benches. Everyone with their ties, white shirts. On the playing field grass. The fence behind us, the school behind the fence. Tall windows. Alan. David. Blair. Duncan. Laura. Anne. Sheila. Spider. All the rest. The teacher to the left. Mrs. Hall. Tweed suit. She feels so old. Everyone smiling into the camera. I'm third from the right in the back row. The smallest boy. The sun in my eyes. It always seems to be in my eyes.

A fight at playtime. Alan Smith versus Alan Thompson. Alan S punches Alan T and down he goes. Alan S is cheered and patted on the back. The crowd drifts away. Alan T gets up with tears running down his face and shouts the questions *What have I done? Why does nobody like me?* The answer, my friend, is blowing in the wind.

Skimming the pond with a green net attached to a cane. Algae and minnows. Drinking cold water from the Barshaw Park fountain. Shuddering about on the witch's hat. Getting dizzy on the roundabout. Hanging on for dear life. Falling over. Flying as high as we can on the swings. Kicking the sky. Twisting and turning the chains of the swing then letting go and spinning spinning spinning to earth. The world moving faster than it's ever moved before.

Mum and dad bought me a pair of binoculars in Scarborough. Black. A cord for the neck. I wanted the hunting set with the silver knife which I noticed after the binoculars had been bought. I threw the binoculars against the pavement and they smashed. I started whimpering. I was too scared to go on the ghost train. I wanted to but I couldn't. The cars vanishing through the swing doors. Dad said *It's okay*. The distant screams and laughter. The dark behind the doors.

Searching in the sand for something on Treasure Island. Anything. I found a doubloon. A pirate must have dropped it when I wasn't looking. Staring through the window of a locked hut with a massive chest inside it brimming with coins and jewels. Red. Silver. Dazzling my eyes. Miniature battleships on a big pond. A castle on a hill. Other places. Dunoon. Walking through the fairy glen at night. Magical coloured bulbs. Holding mum's hand. Little figures perched on toadstools. The Trees. Dark. The bright windows of the guest house. A giant book in a Scottish cave. A scarecrow sitting in a boat in a field. Pulling its oars in an unbelievable sea. A tide of images.

Really angry about something. Angry with mum and dad. Something dumb. Couldn't get my way. Standing halfway up the stairs looking over the banister at mum and dad looking up. Trying hard to think of the most awful thing I could say to make them feel bad. *You big ..... You big ..... You big PUFFY PUFF!* That was it. My best shot. Mum and dad killing themselves laughing. Me charging up to my room.

Cartoons and creaky cowboys at the cinema. Wearing our ABC Minors badges. Kids screaming and shouting and stamping their feet. Kids up on the stage dancing in a long line to Then I Kissed Her by the Beach Boys. A girl twisting at the right hand side. I didn't dance. Dad bought the song for me afterwards. My first piece of vinyl.

It was discovered I was good at drawing so dad took me to a Saturday morning art club for children at Paisley Museum. A room to the left just inside the entrance. Drawing animals and birds. Drawing creatures brought from glass cases. I only went once. I'd rather find the way on my own.

We were too old for cuddly toys. We'd throw panda against the wall. Tie him to mum's footstool and torture him. Eventually we pulled his eyes out. His time was up. Gordon would then throw me against the couch, but not too hard. It was a laugh. A ritual. Something to do. To make him attack I'd wrap my arms around his legs and say *My idol!* or *I am God's messenger, do your worst!* I wasn't. He did.

Someone on the street getting married. Kids waiting for the bride to leave. Jostling for position. Suddenly coins thrown into the air and down onto the road and it's a mad scramble as we push and shove and crawl around and grab what we can as the car pulls away it's every man for himself no prisoners taken. Sixpences and shillings and threepenny bits. Money for nothing.

Mum and dad at work. Gran looking after us. We're out of control. Jumping about. Too much. Not listening. Gran asking us to calm down and stop it. *Now stop it. Come on boys.* Not listening. Laughing, fighting with a red snake belt. Whipping it about. Too much. Out of control. *Come on boys.* The belt stretching back and flying forward and hitting gran on the face. The eye. We run up the stairs. Scared. Too much. Silent. Wait for a while and look over the banister. Gran on the chair in the corner. Her face in her hands. Silently crying. Rhythmic sobs. Breaths. After a while we come down. Stand in front of her. *Are you okay gran? We're sorry gran. We didn't mean it.* We're scared. *Are you okay gran? We're sorry.* She didn't tell.

We went to see Zulu. The red jackets. The white helmets. The blue sky. The thumping of spears against shields. The figures on the hillside looking down at me. The middle of everywhere. The burning hospital. The cinema full of fathers and sons. Males eating ice cream and drinking Kia-Ora. Warriors singing. We went home and re-enacted the final charge. REAR RANK, FIRE! Heaps of black bodies in our back garden. Time for tea.

Our class taking possession of the bushes at the edge of the playground as if this was of crucial importance and then a big charge in a long line by children from the rest of the school to claim the bushes back like some dramatic last stand in a battle maybe we'd been watching too many movies or something but there they are charging at us as we make a brave but ultimately thrillingly meaningless defence as if what we were playing at had some meaning.

Playing in the bushes on the waste ground. A smear of jobby on Ron Morton's underpants. He couldn't help it. Couldn't make it home in time. He took them off and showed it to me. I'm not sure why. I didn't particularly want to look.

A birthday party and everyone's here. All my friends. Lots of presents. Lamps burning. It's going well. Jelly and crisps and other things. Ron Morton makes me angry. He's having fun without me in another room. It's as if I believe I don't exist. I'm jealous. Soon everyone has to gather for the blowing out of the candles. As they come in I point at Ron who stands with outstretched arms and a look of astonishment. *Everyone except HIM!*

A new extension being built for the primary school. The workers outside their hut drinking tea from cans with thin wire handles. Dumper trucks in July. Cement mixers. Wheelbarrows. We'd cross the plank bridge over the burn rolling putty in our hands. A smell of something sickly sweet. Burning braziers. We'd walk around in the primitive building when the workers had gone home. Balance along the joists. Get splinters in our fingers. A young workie had long hair and looked like the singer from The Tremeloes. The girls would follow him about. One day I peeped around the corner of the hut and a huge stone smashed into my nose. I walked home with blood coming out and Ron Morton telling me to *Be a brave boy, Graham, be a brave boy.* Being brave was the last thing on my mind.

The garage. The thick smell of wood, sun, dustlight, silence. Toboggans hanging from nails. A coal scuttle. A Hillman Minx lubrication chart. A Coronation tea tin full of washers, screws, pieces of metal. Listening for something. An old knife covered in paint. A watering can. A lawnmower. A hoe, a spade, a rake. A tin of oil. A metal bucket. A trowel caked with earth. A wireless box from World War Two. Headphones. A cobbler's last that belonged to someone gone. A No. 40 washboard. Cobwebs on the windows. The door closing behind me as I leave.

Along the path between the building and the wall. Up the stone steps and left into the reception. Name. Appointment time. Into the waiting room. Trying to read a comic. Looking at Punch. The door opening and someone's name being called. Not mine. Waiting. Hoping the dentist suddenly takes ill. My name. Into the room and into the seat and looking at the science fiction lamp over my head and the tumbler of pink liquid and the display of evil implements waiting. Fast drill. Slow drill. The little mirror and the thin pick. Mr. Paterson looking at files. No turning back. Swallowing in panic. One time I refused to go in and stood looking out the big waiting room window with the nurse's arm around my shoulder. Dad bought me a TV21 comic to cheer me up. Once I was given gas and it was all over before I knew it and I laughed with delight. A rare occasion. It's always worse than you imagine it to be.

A big flat lollipop stick placed on my tongue. Making me gag. A wart on my knee. Doctor McGeogh with the menacing stethoscope around his neck distracts me. When I look the other way he stabs in a long sharp point. I scream. It seems the right thing to do.

Toast on Saturday evening. The winter. Four of us around the coal fire. Warmth. Television. Thick slices of white bread on a long two-pronged fork. A fancy carved handle. Handed down from someone to someone. The bread on the points, held out against the flames. We'd watch it becoming golden, being turned, removed at just the right time. Not too dark, not too light. Perfect symmetry. Nothing has ever tasted as good. Mum would spread the butter. We'd get one each, wait our turn, eat, wait for the next. We didn't want it to stop. The fork. The flames. The bread. Gordon. Mum. Dad. Me.

Through the kitchen door and into the dining room. Dining table to the left. Dark wood with a half moon flap. Chairs in the corners. Window looking onto the garden. Ship in a bottle on the sill made by a German prisoner of war. Old grey metal fire with thin sparking elements and a dark wood sideboard full of plates, a cake stand, cups and saucers. Napkins and tablecloths. Black place mats with a pattern. Over to the right a red trolley on wheels. The glass sliding doors that open into the lounge.

Tired. Unable to sleep. Christmas Eve. Reaching down into the dark to see if the big football sock is full yet. Gordon and me, a sock each. Still flat. Empty. Mum peeping round the door. Unable to sleep. Reaching down. Empty, flat. Unable to sleep. Falling asleep. Waking up. Reaching down into the darkness. The sock. Full. Lumpy. Full of shapes. The Rangers sock. An orange at the bottom. Resisting the need to see what's there. Really there. Falling asleep. Asleep. Not waking. Really asleep.

I'm going with Anne Linn to Alan Hume's birthday party. Everyone thinks it's a great idea if I give her a red rose as I get into Mr. Linn's car. I'm not so sure. Do I have to? I hand it over anyway. Everyone chuckles. I gave Sheila Smart a handmade card on Valentine's Day. Mum helped me make it. Unrequited first loves.

A dwarf walked from door to door selling combs and shoelaces and shoe polish on Saturday nights. I'd sit at the bedroom window and watch for him at the top of the hill. Watch him as he went from door to door. The amount of time he took at each door telling me if he'd sold anything or not. His brown tatty suitcase. Any weather. He'd reach us and ring the bell. I'd stand behind dad's legs and look at him. A grown-up about my size. He'd smile. He seemed to know what I was thinking. I didn't know what I was thinking. Dad would always buy something even if we didn't need it. He knew it's what I wanted. It helped. Eventually he never came back. I watched for a while then stopped. *Is it true what mummy said, you won't come back? Oh no no.*

Sometimes we couldn't go home at lunchtime. We had to eat our sandwiches in the temporary prefab classroom with Mrs. Hubner as she did her marking. Silent. Mrs. Hubner tried to get me to change from left hand to right hand. She gave up after a short while. Mrs. Hubner was the mother of someone called Billy Raymond. He was famous. She liked telling us how famous he was. Other times in the holidays we went to gran's house or gran would come to ours or we'd stay in alone and promise to behave and sometimes we'd go to mum's work and be there all day. Mum was a comptometer operator for Allied Suppliers. Working out the wages in a blue overall. People doing their jobs. The jobs I couldn't imagine doing. I would never be that old.

I went to Duncan MacFadyen's house for some reason after school. Over Buchlyvie and down to the Glasgow Road and across the road to other roads and finally the road where he lived. His house. It seemed so far from home. The front gate. A long way from what I knew. The bluebell woods at the top of Kinpurnie was far as well. Playing below the leaves. Searching for conkers. Searching the golf course for golf balls and selling them back to the golfers. The unknown regions. A flat earth I could tumble off.

The baths across from the cattle pens and the smell of cold drinks in the warm damp of the entrance. Going from cold to heat and back again. Trunks inside a rolled-up towel. The smell of chlorine. Cubicles with wooden doors. Swimming lessons for the useless. Me. Boys and girls in a line at the edge of the shallow end. I was asked to jump. A long way down. I did. Entered. The water went over my head. Light submerged. It went up my nose. In my eyes. Bubbling and flooding. I thrashed about. Never returned. Bought fish and chips from the shop next door.

Through the car wash tunnel with the whooshing water and the slopping soap and the noise of the brushes and the strangeness in a moving safe box. Like a submarine submerging. Wondering what would happen if the water started to get in. Would we drown? Nobody hearing our cries for help. The car slowly filling up. Suddenly out in the light. The last trickles on the window panes. All clean. The suds of moments.

A lift with a black concertina grill you pull across.   Up
through the centre of the stairwell.   Into a large top floor
space with huge rolls of cloth and men cutting and machines
running. We're having little suits made for a wedding. Dad
gets them at a discount from one of his customers.   Our
bodies are measured and marks are made with chalk. At the
wedding there's a tiny fragile little girl, almost brittle, whose
hand I take as she slowly goes up the stairs then slowly
comes down the stairs.   The right foot leading with each
step taken.   I watch her carefully.   I've never seen anyone
like her.   I want to help.   There must be something wrong.
People were married and we went home.

The pavements are full of ghosts.   Halloween.   I was an
Arab with a rifle and a little moustache which mum drew
on my face.   I was an old woman and Graham Brown was
my husband.   We stayed in character and spoke with old
voices in neighbours' living rooms.   I walked with a stick.
Imagined what it was like to be too old. We read a poem and
dooked for apples and filled our bags with threepenny bits
and monkey nuts.   The last time Gordon and myself walked
around with sheets over us and plastic skeleton masks bought
from the ironmonger.   Two little Deaths gliding soundlessly
around the streets.   Knocking on doors.   *Let us in*.

An alcove in the corner of the lounge with a lamp and ornaments. A cheap china lady with a blue skirt. Penguins. A cupboard beneath full of thick 78 records, a booklet with the Seven Wonders of the World inside it. Miniature Spanish dictionaries. A concertina. Cowboy scrapbook. Queen's Coronation souvenir magazine. A carpet, a rug, a three piece suite. A dark wood cigarette stand. Hearth. Fire. Mantelpiece. Clock. Ticking. A dark wood bookcase full of books. The Great War - I Was There. Swiss Family Robinson. The Pampas and the Andes. Tschiffely's Ride. Little busts of Beatrice and Dante on top. The Duomo of Florence brought back from the war. A television in the corner. A shiny bell from Chile. A window looking onto the street. Coffee table. Record player. Vinyl in a rack. TV Century 21 Themes. Mozart. The Black and White Minstrels. Ragtime Cowboy Joe. Val Doonican. I'm a Believer. Letters in a rack. A tasseled standard lamp with the scuffed base we'd ram our toy cars against.

I went on and on about it. *I want Action Man.* Eventually mum went out and bought me Combat Johnny from the ironmonger. It was dark. She went out to get it before it closed. Pinned on the wall between the pots and pans. A puny plastic warrior. Head too big. Body too small. I wanted Action Man with his perfect proportions. The closest she could get. It was dark. I looked at it with contempt. Cannon fodder. Never played with it. Threw it under the bed.

I slipped on the ice of a frozen pond and thumped my head. A Desperate Dan-type lump came up on my skull. Beneath my hair. No hesitation. One second it wasn't there and the next it was. I didn't know water could feel so hard.

I went into the garden on the morning after bonfire night and picked up all of the fireworks I could find and put them in a shoe box. All the dead Bangers. The Roman Candles and Fountains. The Rockets that flew then fell to earth. Every colour you can think of. The cold gunpowder in my nose. Safe in the daylight. I didn't trust fireworks. They seemed sly. I'd cower well back, sometimes hold a sparkler in my glove and watch dad lighting the blue touch paper with a Catherine Wheel shrieking and spinning against the side of the coal bunker. The noise of a mad world. I dumped them in the bin. Let them go.

The light at the top of the stairs stank of fish. No reason we could think of. Electricity gone bad.

Ice on the inside of our bedroom window. Dad's shape in the doorway. Dad saying five minutes more. *Five minutes more.* Then up. Quickly. A shivering wash in the bathroom. Mum making breakfast. Then out into the fog, or the snow. Whatever it happened to be that day. Balaclavas over our heads. The school day darkness. Headlights carefully along the road. We were close enough to walk. Past the palings. Past the railings. The gate and the children moving around. Phantoms. Our own breaths. Waiting for the bell to take us inside.

Doing the Grand Old Duke of York. Doing the Hokey Cokey. Going in and out. Backwards and forwards. Dancing in circles holding hands. Avril McQueen had a wart on her palm. Musical chairs. Frantic games. I won the pass the parcel contest. First prize. A huge tube of Smarties. I didn't want to let it go.

Gordon brought home a Guinea Pig called Ginger from school. It made strange bleeping noises. We made a maze of Annuals for him to run around in. Probably terrified. We killed ourselves laughing. My class had a hamster called Sally. We looked at her in her cage or on her wheel or under her straw. Hard pellets. The wheel going round. Bright black eyes. Stuffed cheeks. We loved her. Alan Hume took her home during the summer holidays to look after her and make sure she stayed alive. At the start of the new term the teacher told us the news. A lot of crying. An introduction to death.

Sports day on the playing field. A set of plastic yellow golf clubs for the winner. A holy grail. Egg and spoon race. Going well, dropped the egg before the end. Finished fourth. Sack Race. Going well, fell over before the end. Finished fourth. Three-legged race. Me and Bracky. We practised hard. One two one two one two one two. Going well, didn't fall over. Finished fourth.

The back door. The wooden garage and wide shallow concrete steps leading down to a small triangle of earth. A use for every limit of space. The two lawns with a path in between. Clothes poles at the side of the garage. The hedge. The bushes and trees at the bottom. A jungle for our Action Men. A world to get lost in. The high wall separating us from Penilee. The other side of the tracks. The crazy paving patio. The fence separating us from our semi-detached neighbours. The rockery with the rocks that dad brought from different places. Converging. The coal bunker. The path below the window. The back door.

Boiling afternoon.   Lots of children in the house and the garden.   No particular reason.   Our turn.   I'm kneeling on the floor of the lounge surrounded by sheets of paper drawing incredibly fast with coloured pencils.   Picture after picture of superheroes. More. More. Faster. Faster. Trying to keep up with demand.   Calling for more paper. Find more paper if you want more heroes.   Batman, Spider-Man, Hawkman, The Torch, Aquaman, Submariner, Silver Surfer, Hawkeye, The Flash, Daredevil, Superman, Fantastic Four, Green Lantern, X-Men, Thor, Captain America, Iron Man, Teen Titans, The Wasp, Ant-Man.   No villains.   Just heroes.   Page after page taken out and pinned on the inside of the garage.   Kids filing in to look.   A strange gallery.   Like a church.   How do I know it really happened?   The pictures are thrown out sometime in the future.   Disposable heroes. Here then gone.

Gordon fired an arrow into his eye.   He was mucking about with a bow in next door's garage.   The stick went the wrong way.   Dad rushed him to hospital and we waited.   Mum and me.   Maybe he's lost an eye.   They came back.   His eye was okay but he had to wear a patch.   He looked like a pirate.   A small Scottish pirate.

A mass of nettles against a high wall at the garages.   Little Triffids.   We'd bring some sticks.   Chop and swish and slash for a long time.   Sweat.   Red.   We saw red.   We got stung. White bumps came up on our skin.   We rubbed them with doaken.   We slashed harder.   Us or them.   It felt good to see the bits flying through the air.   Slow motion.   Like a film.   A battlefield.   Broken stalks and chopped up leaves.   I'd come back on my own and do some more.   They didn't seem to mind, grew back in the same place when we weren't looking.

Dad.   Working on the car in the garage.   Me, watching.   He asks me to put my foot on a pedal.   Wants to check something, see what the matter is.   I press too much.   The roar fills the garage.   The vibration of something ancient.   Dad shouts. He never shouts.   I run into the house, probably start crying, never learn to drive.

On the bike in the back garden.   Two wheels for the first time. No stabilisers.   No three wheeler.   Wobbling about.   Dad keeping me steady then letting go.   Suddenly I'm moving on my own.   Just me.   Perfect balance.   In a circle on the lawn.   I feel high up.   Something has changed and there's no return.

Dad's repertoire of sneezes. A big YEEEEESH, followed by two restrained TEE-WEH-TAH TEE-WEH-TAH, followed by a small world-weary OHHHH, and all rounded off with a gigantic WAAAHOOOO! We'd create a little rhythmic routine comprising these sounds and sing it back to him at the dinner table. He must have been thrilled. He also had a varicose vein that he told us was shrapnel and a filling in a tooth we would point at and say *Glinto!*

Things in the kitchen. The pulley above our heads. Cod liver oil. Malt. Blue bottles of Milk of Magnesia. Vick. Daz. Ajax. Fairy Liquid. Palmolive. Eggs. Egg cups with Noddy on them. Haliborange tablets. Tupperware. Bags of brown sugar. Soup. A wooden spoon for stirring the soup. A rolling pin. A bowl for mixing cakes. A spoon for mixing cakes we could lick. Thick heavy cooking pots. Made to last a lifetime. Sliced bread. A metal bin with the word BREAD on it in green letters. Shreddies. Ricicles. Heinz tins. Spam. Homepride flour. Angel Delight. Bisto. Oxo. Ritz Crackers. Bird's Eye fish fingers. Nesquik. Eat Me dates. Jaffa cakes. Dairylea triangles. Tree Top fruit squash. Fizzy drinks in bottles. Milk in bottles with red tops. An electric cooker. Tins of Creamola Foam. Just add water and stir. Mum's apron. Brave new luxuries. Back door. Window.

Sitting in the row of seats at the barber. Waiting our turn. Hair of men all over the floor. The boss and the young guy and the wee smiling man with the hooky nose. My favourite. He got the children's seat and placed it across the grown-up seat so I could be higher and see myself in the mirror. Scissors and creams and plug-in razors. Photographs on the walls of young men with gravity-defying hair styles. Hair for the space age. You too can look like this!

Nothing to do. Switching on the television. Waiting for something to happen. Early afternoon. Blankness. Silence. The beginning of a distant music. Slowly building to a crescendo. A triumphant Scottish marching tune. The STV logo. We were easily pleased.

Mum in the kitchen making me beans on toast. Telling me all about this film she saw at the pictures where a woman looks through a pair of binoculars and a pair of spikes go into her eyes. She said it was horrible. I believed her. Telling me all about a man not too long ago called Christie who murdered women and hid them behind a wall in his kitchen. He looked really creepy. Little spectacles. Telling me all about someone who put women in a bath of acid. Brilliant!

A horse and cart collecting stuff.   Anything nobody wants.
The horse clopping up the road.   The dustbin men emptying
the old metal bins.   Clattering and banging.   Dirty faces,
dirty hands.   Mum saying *If you don't do well at school you'll end
up just like them*.   The blue and white mobile dairy with the
steps at the back going up to the counter.   Stuffy heat.   The
smell of tins.   Metal and dust.   Buying some fizzy drink and
a packet of crisps with a little blue bag of salt then sneaking
back on when the driver starts it up and hitching a lift to the
top of the crescent.   Walking back down.

Andy Pandy on strings.   Teddy going mental.   Looby Loo
dancing about.   The Woodentops.   Spotty Dog.   Bill and Ben.
Weed.   Tales from the Riverbank.   Doctor Who.   William Tell.
Champion the Wonder Horse.   Supercar.   Mike Mercury.
Fireball XL5.   Steve Zodiac.   Zoony the Lazoon.   Stingray.
The hubbly bubbly Aquaphibians.   Thunderbirds.   Captain
Pugwash.   Noggin the Nog.   Nogbad the Bad.   Christopher
Trace.   John Noakes.   Bleep and Booster.   Animal Magic.
The Tinderbox.   Vision On.   Sooty.   Jackanory.   Zokko.
Gigantor.   Daktari.   Pinky and Perky.   Crackerjack.   Tingha
and Tucker.   Yogi Bear.   Top Cat.   Deputy Dawg.   Zebedee.
Kaboobie the flying camel.   Marine Boy.   Hergé's Adventures
of Tintin.   Jonny Quest.   The Flintstones.   How.   Rawhide.
Bonanza.   Take Your Pick.   David Nixon.   Basil Brush.   The
Dick Van Dyke Show.   Casey Jones.   Flipper.   Hector's House.
Belle and Sebastian.   Lost in Space.   Captain Scarlet.   The
Mysterons.   The Munsters.   The Addams Family.   Pilgrim's
Progress.   Scary television sets coming to life on the Benny
Hill Show.   Sitting on the carpet throughout the 60s.

The ice cream vans. Porrellis. Red and off-white. Jimmy the Icey in his grey coat and brylcreemed hair. Orange and white. They came at different times. They'd stop at the top of the hill, then come down and stop halfway. We'd watch from the window and dive out when we saw it moving towards us. The tune playing. Kids pouring out of their doors. Survival of the fittest. Ice cream cones with raspberry sauce. Oysters and 99s. Ice lollies. Monkees cards. Outer Limits cards. World War Two cards. Planet of the Apes cards. But mostly American Civil War bubble gum cards. Pictures of people having their legs blown off or a bayonet stuck in their guts. We'd swap for the ones we didn't have. A man with a bloody bandage around his head. A man screaming as he's crushed by a rolling wheel. What was a Civil War? What was America? Was it something from the past or something imagined? Only another thirty three to get.

We taught a wee boy in the street to run around saying *Rebel Power!* over and over again. Like a parrot. It was one of the captions on a Civil War card. Over and over to whoever would listen. Children. Grown-ups. Even we got sick of it after a while. We also taught someone else to say *I'll get the Pterodactyl to you!* for some reason lost in the mist of history. We were older and wiser and had to show the youngsters the way. Show them how to behave in public.

Two channels on the television. Grainy pictures. A school in Wales. Men on a mountain of mud. A place called Aberfan. The faces of murderers staring from the screen. A woman with blonde hair. A young man. They killed some children. Mum held us closer. A war on the other side of the world in a jungle. American soldiers. Somebody called Vietcong. Somebody called Mad Mitch. A politician lying on the floor of a hotel. A place called Biafra. Skeleton children with huge eyes and bloated stomachs. Black runners holding up black fists. People throwing things in Paris. People throwing things in Northern Ireland. Too far to understand. Can I go out to play? Get on with life.

Sitting in the front row of the pictures giggling and gabbing and rustling wrappers and eating Aztec or Milky Way or Chocolate Buttons or Macaroon Bars or Mars or Picnic or Toffee Crisp or Opal Fruits fresh with the tang of sickness or Fruit Polos or Bounty or Peppermint or Fry's Five Centre or Fry's Cream or Dairy Milk or Rainbow Drops or Jelly Babies or Aero or Mint Aero or Skippy or Treets or Peanut Treets or Extra or Spangles or Milky Bar or Revels or Munchies or Mintola or Toffo or Fruit Gums or Caramac or Bar Six or Galaxy or Golden Cup or Crunchie or Fudge or Flake or Ripple or Turkish Delight or Topic or Maltesers or Dairy Crunch or Fruit and Nut or Rolo or Smarties and all the others that had never existed until now and trying not to puke.

Making machine gun noises with our mouths. DRRRRROW!
Japs and Commandos. Dead serious. We knew about the
war from our dads. Playing with Action Man in the back
garden. Building forts out of house bricks. Defensive
positions in the bushes. Some in German uniforms carrying
German guns, throwing German grenades. Others in British
uniforms carrying British guns. A medic on stand-by to care
for the wounded. Spending hours setting up armies of tiny
Airfix soldiers only to mow them down in an instant. The
bloodlust satisfied.

The Victor. The Hotspur. TV21. Fantastic. Terrific. Lying
in bed, reading our comics. Sitting on the back step, reading
our comics. Sprawling on the lawn, reading our comics.
Sitting on a neighbour's doorstep, reading our comics. The
Dandy, The Beezer, The Beano, The Topper. Commando
Books. *Englander pig dog. Banzai!* In the endless sixties
sunlight. The smell of cut grass. White butterflies. Fat
buzzing bees. Drinking Creamola Foam. Drinking ginger
beer. Eating bread and butter and sugar. Paper turning.

Dad took us to Gourock to play at the edge of the sea. Our Action Men dressed in rubber suits. Masks. Flippers. Oxygen tanks. One with an orange lifejacket on. Pretending they were on a World War mission to blow something up. Scrambling them up the side of rocks and pushing them off. They never drowned. Always came back for more. Expressions never changing. Fearless. Dad took our black and white pictures with his small brown camera. Wading in pools the tide left behind. Sinking our hands inside the cold Clyde.

Gordon deciding to climb the sea wall at Crail. Me following. Without thinking. It had to be done. A vertical wall. I'll be dead if I fall. I can see it. My body in shorts, T-shirt, sandals, socks. Floating face down. A moment. No bother for Gordon, up and away. Only me, alone, clinging to the wall. Two feet from the top. Frozen. I look down. I look at the wall. I look up. The sea, the stone, the sky. Two arms reaching down and grabbing my wrists and pulling me up and onto the ground. The blink of an eye. An off-duty policeman. Passing by. Gone. Mum and dad didn't know until it was all over. We gave them the slip. It had to be done. Without thinking.

Picnic lunch packed. Tartan thermos flask packed. Car rug on the back seat. Transistor radio. Beezer Summer Special. Sweets for mum to pop in dad's mouth. Dad checking the water is switched off and the plugs are out. The milk's been cancelled. Normal life's been cancelled. The doors locked and checked. Into the Anglia and away to Ardfern. Free. There was a small rip in the lining of the car in the back and moths kept flying out. A gateway from somewhere else. Once a strange big orange insect with wings was on the window and it freaked us out. Dimensions overlapping.

The crowd standing about at Inverary. Trying to get a better view of Para Handy with his sunglasses on. Sunny Jim with his wee bunnet. The Vital Spark tied to the pier. A lull in the filming. I was too shy and didn't want to go up close. I didn't want to be noticed. Started to cry. Gran was there to say *Never mind son*. Later on we got our photos taken with John Grieve. Smiling with our Batman badges. His friendly hands on our shoulders. The sky grey. The summer starting. Again.

Past Lochgilphead and past Dunadd and all the Neolithic tombs at Kilmartin and we're into cowboy country. The hills crowding in around us. Indians massing in the passes. Waiting to attack. The forts on the summits. And then the road curving down. The familiar feeling of expectation. A tantalising glimpse and suddenly Loch Craignish is stretched out before us to our left. The islands. The boats. The special water. Ardfern village. Our cottage too far to see but we know is there. The gate. The path. The radio playing The Day I Met Marie. The handle waiting to be turned. The beds waiting to be slept in. The windows waiting to be opened.

Down the dirt track to the stone jetty. The rickety old
boatshed full of lifejackets and skis and ropes and nets and
things for the water. Along to the very edge to peer down
and see starfish or crabs or rockhoppers or tiny swishing fish
in the deep clear water and unwind our crab lines and plop
them in and wait for something to grab hold or bite. Lob
rocks at the jellyfish. Wobble about laughing on the square
red raft attached to the jetty by a dripping rope. Tom Sawyer
and Huckleberry Finn. One time dad was on the raft and
tried to haul it back to the jetty but fell in. Dad going one
way and the raft going the other. Great. One time I was so
demented to be there I ran straight into the loch and flooded
my boots. We'd only arrived five minutes before and I was
already sodden. Ridiculous. Wonderful.

We took the boat with the small white sail. Set off from the jetty and were soon out of sight. Beyond the first island. Behind the second. Steady progress. No sense of danger. We hadn't told anyone. Gordon, our pal Kevin, and me. Kevin knew what he was doing. Knew how to sail a boat. Black seal heads peeped above the water watching then dipped down to appear somewhere else watching. Lumps in the water. It was warm. Calm. Dreamlike. The loch belonged to us. The sun going down. We arrived at the jetty on the second island. Ran about in the trees. No thought of hurrying to get back. No thought that it would soon be dark. A speed boat suddenly roared up. There was a massive search going on. They expected to find our bodies but found us still alive instead. It zipped us back to Ardfern. The restless wake behind us. I don't know who brought back our boat with the sail. I expect the seals were watching.

The gulls were nesting. We ran all over their tiny island and up and down throwing rocks at them. We hit some. A small coil of guts spilled out onto a rock. I threw an egg hard onto the ground. I thought it would burst all yolky like the eggs we ate. There was a little pink-blue creature sleeping tight inside with veins on its unhatched unready flesh. I killed it. I stood and stared. I ran. Lord of the Flies. My favourite book.

There was a butterfly in our cottage bedroom. A tortoiseshell. We looked it up in the I-Spy book. Mesmerising. A painting with wings. We put a tumbler over it and went to sleep. We'll let it go in the morning. It was dead. We dropped it out of the window into the sunlight. It fell to the flowers below.

I went seriously up to an old gentleman standing at the end of the jetty who was wearing a deerstalker hat and holding a stick and looking sadly out onto the water and gazed up at him and said *Tell us about the rabbits George, and tell us about the chickens George, and tell us about living off the fat of the land* which was from Of Mice and Men which dad was reading then turned and walked seriously away as he smiled in amazement.

We drove along the side of the loch to Craignish Point. Oystercatchers peeping. A metal gate barred our way. I got out and opened it and the car drove through. I closed it and walked back to the car. As I reached the door the car drove off. Drove about twenty yards. I walked up casually and got to the door again and it drove off. Drove about twenty yards. The third time I reached the door and got in. We were all laughing. We did it every time but it never failed. Knew what was coming. A sacred ritual. Divine expectation.

A café in Oban. Or somewhere near Oban. A group of young long haired men and women at a table. Drinking coffee. Smoking cigarettes. This May Be The Last Time playing on the radio.

Thursday. Dad upstairs. Mum in the kitchen. Top of the Pops on the telly. Jimmy Savile surrounded by young girls. A hole in my shoe, something in the air, flowers in the rain. The Move singing about the Fire Brigade. Gran shocked by the onslaught of hair. The faces filling the screen. Jumping Jack Flash. All You Need Is Love. The countdown from 30 to 1. If Paradise Was Half As Nice. Itchycoo Park. Someone singing about Grocer Jack. Someone singing about Kites, Balloons, Everlasting Love. Mighty Quinn, Spirits In The Sky. Someone singing about how we're going to burn. Julie Driscoll with asylum eyes. A place called San Francisco. A long way from Paisley.

Rounders in the street until it got dark. A tennis racquet for a bat. Chalk circles for homes. Round and round. The ball tumbling down the road. Hardly any cars. Hopscotch and skipping for the girls. Hide and Seek in the gardens. Dead Man's Fall for the boys. Pretending to be shot and the best death wins. Statues. Moving forward then holding still. Running at a line of linked arms. Last man standing. Trying to break through to another side.

The Cybermen on the moon. The Cybermen in the snow. William Hartnell turning into Patrick Troughton. People going all black and white and electrocuted when a Dalek exterminates them. A strange gathering of evil scary monsters round a huge evil table. Plotting nasty things. The sound the Tardis makes when it vanishes or appears. The sound it makes when it's standing still. Thinking. The Zarbi and the Menoptra. Quarks and Chumblies. Men in dodgy ant costumes. Ice Warriors hissing. Yeti shuffling along underground stations. A man in a jungle pricked by a thorn and slowly being covered in cotton wool as he screams. Watching from behind whatever's available.

The big hedge in the back garden. Ten feet tall. I'd search through the dark fairy tale tangle until I found an unguarded nest. A beautiful construction of little bits and twigs. Small and perfect. Sometimes there would be eggs. A strange shade of greeny-blue with speckles. I'd lift them out and look at them and put them back. I worried in case the mother was watching and wouldn't return. In case I'd ruined it.

Gordon joined the cricket club but was out for a duck and never went back. He was a cub and then he was a scout. I heard the words Akela and Sixer being used. During the scout fête he tried to beat the St. Mirren goalie Jim Thorburn but didn't quite make it. Three shots. Into his hands. He wore boots with badger and fox prints on the sole and went to a camp called Peesweep. Away for days. Character building. Searching. He once dressed up as a policeman. I don't know why.

Graham Henry was bullying me in the playground after school. Gordon tried to stop him. Protect me. Graham Henry got him on the ground and was hitting him on the head and laughing. I couldn't help. His dad's big dog did a big jobby on our lawn. Stinking. Brown. Our dad scooped it up and marched down to his house and dumped it in their porch. All before school. It didn't happen again. We won.

Into Paisley on the red bus you jumped on at the back. The
Variety Stores to look at the latest toys. Then along to the
Yankee Mags shop. Down a side street. A Fort Knox of
American comics. The best. Piles and piles. Action Comics.
Harvey Comics. Casper the Friendly Ghost. Richie Rich.
Archie Comics. DC and Marvel full of real people like The
Lizard, The Green Goblin, Brainiac, The Vulture, Doctor
Octopus, Doctor Doom, The Mandarin, Red Skull, Sandman,
The Blob, The Grey Gargoyle, The Joker, The Riddler, The
Penguin, Scarecrow, Catwoman, Toad, Loki, Magneto. A
world full of villains at our fingertips. The sunshine and the
pictures and the smell of paper. Read them for ages and buy
nothing. No one bothered.

We sometimes had to go and visit people and they sometimes
came to us. Iain and Anne Stewart. Dad's best man. They
had a son who was a genius who said *You want to play with
you now?* instead of *You want to play with me now?* He could
calculate the size of the universe in his head. Sheila and
John Wallace. Friends from years ago. They were nice. I'd
sit behind their couch and draw all night. They didn't mind.
Jack and Rita Norris. I don't know who they were. They
had a retriever called Honey that splashed in the sea and a
daughter with a picture of the Beach Boys on her bedroom
wall. Ian and Betty Fulton. The last of dad's relatives. They
had a hand grenade as a doorstop and an old woman called
Aunt Nora who made snorting noises. She probably wasn't
too keen on us either.

Granny Fulton's house. Far off in Glasgow. Up sad stone steps and into a dim room with high ceilings. Old furniture. Dark wardrobes and dainty cups. A smell of mothballs. A smell of an old world getting older. Dad talking to his mum about how things are. How things used to be. What's happened and what's going to happen. Us waiting to go home. In the corridor outside, the steps down to the scary basement stank of wee-wee. Granny Fulton stayed with us at home for a while. Lived upstairs in mum and dad's bedroom. We'd go and visit her. It was only for a while and then she was gone.

Granny Fulton said we were descended from the pirate Captain Kidd. Her name before she became Fulton was Kidd. Captain Kidd was born in Scotland. Good enough for us. All the proof we needed. Captain Pugwash was never the same again.

I'm drawing on paper on the carpet. Drawing the Jupiter 2 from Lost in Space. Concentrating. Getting it right. Someone hanging in space. Hundreds and hundreds of stick soldiers copied from Civil War bubblegum cards. Each one in his proper place. Drawing fish in an old folks' home. A ring of old women. Watching me. A fresh life. All of them smiling. Granny Fulton one of them. Me at the beginning. Them at the end.

The straight back wood of the High Church pew.   Same place every week.   Old people in their best coats and hats. Gran. Aunt Isa. A man's shiny bald head in the row in front. Collection plates. Babies being christened. At half time the children trooped to the hall next door for things about God. Sunday school songs. Jesus loves me. Tell me the old old story.   A picture of Goliath being whacked on the head in my bible. Sometimes we had to wait for ages afterwards as dad helped with the collections. Portraits of dead ministers staring down.   I drew a picture of EARTH and MERCURY and SUN and a man being shot on the bottom with an arrow on the inside page of my hymn book. Hell to pay.

On the braes above Paisley.   The car in the car park. Scrambling about on the rocks. Charging up and down in the high grass. Energy unending. The smell of the air. The rush of the sky. A fenced-off culvert that looks like a grave. Our town stretched out below us.   Smokestacks and high flats. A view where we live.

The Beatles doing Penny Lane on Top of the Pops. Yet again. A film of them riding about on horses in a park. Sitting at a table in red jackets. I thought it was boring. Took them for granted. It was the 60s. You don't know what you've got till it's gone.

Still against the wall. Dad placing a long brown ruler flat against my head. Keep still. Don't move. Look straight ahead. Drawing a line with a pen. Marking in blue how much I've changed since the last line was drawn. My height. Blue on white. Blue pen on white paint. Quarter of an inch above the last line which is quarter of an inch above the one below. The past, moving slowly. What I was and what I'm still to be. Gordon's lines beside mine. Parallel universes. Keeping still, travelling through time.

We had a Commando book about 'non-combatants'. People who didn't fight on the front line in World War Two. We then called dad a non-combatant because he was only a lorry driver. Only. Because he wasn't taking part in hand to hand combat. Firing bazookas at German tanks. Storming machine gun nests single-handed with grenades and saving the day. It was just a joke but we didn't know better. He didn't reply. Just smiled. Nodded. He knew his head could have been blown off like anybody else. No big deal. A quiet hero.

The new Cortina pulling into the driveway. Granny McLardie getting out of the passenger side. Slowly. Her coat, hat, shoes. Sunday smart. A bit tired. Always there, smiling, always going to be there. Of course. Nothing remarkable, no one remarkable. These seconds. Always going to be there. Me waving at the window. Gran.

I wanted a Batman outfit for my Action Man. Gran knitted me one with blue wool. A perfect little blue Batman suit for a miniature human being. It must have taken ages. I said *Thank you gran*. I hardly used it. It wasn't the right colour. A thing of magic.

An inter-school quiz. The final in Foxbar. We're there to support our team. In the car park I say *I wonder if old Beggo is coming?* to the person beside me. *So that's what they call me? I always wondered.* Mr. Begg was right behind us. He heard it all. I wanted to die. Our team thrashed them.

Parents' night. Mr. Begg said that I showed a real talent for writing stories and there was a good sense of humour running through them. A story about an underpaid magic carpet salesman and his genie in particular. Mum and dad were proud. I was proud. Mr. Begg was sacked.

Craig Morrison fancied Lesley MacFadyen. He tried to seduce her with a selection box at Christmas. Left it on her doorstep in Roffey Park Road. I tagged along. Encouraged him. The next morning she came in with a face like thunder and dumped it on his desk. She couldn't stand him. I was off the hook. Wasn't even mentioned.

Dad reassured me there would be lots of presents. I asked him how many. Lots and lots. More than seven? Much more than seven. I was worried in case there wouldn't be enough. In the morning there was enough. I looked out of the lounge window and saw a knight charging up the street on an invisible horse.

Things in the classroom. A poster on the wall that said South Yemen. The smell of white chalk. The smell of the duster. White inkwells full of blue ink. Grey socks. Plasticine. A desk with a lid. Milk in a bottle and a straw to drink it. Little blue bean bags for the gym hall. Mrs. Brady reading Wee Macgreegor. Everyone laughing. Lynn Cameron known as Spider who was rubbish at everything. Sums I couldn't do. Long division. Reading the nine times table out loud. Mrs. Brady watching to see who wasn't moving their lips. Pounds, shillings and pence. Gallons, quarts and pints. Ounces, pounds and tons. Red ticks. Gold stars. The report card. Satisfactory. Poor. Must try harder. The corner for someone to stand in. 11 plus. A pole with a hook on the end to open or close the windows. The glass. The sun. The outside.

Mrs. Brady made me stand up and do the sums that were on the blackboard. Seven times eight is. Eight times nine is. I cried. Elaine Skinner looking at me. Cameron Forbes smirking. Everyone quiet. Nine times nine is. It went on forever. I struggled to the end, sat down. Stupid. I sat at a desk at the back of the class. I needed glasses. I couldn't read the chalk. I didn't tell anyone.

In the gym hall doing leapfrog.   Half the boys in a circle waiting to be leapt over.   The other half doing the leaping. The girls watching.   I'm the best by a mile.   I feel like I'm flying.   Everyone open-mouthed with astonishment.   Even Mrs. Brady.   She says *Well, it's obvious who was the best there!* I felt like a star.   I must have hollow bones.   The bones of a bird.

A school trip to another place.   Singing *Ten Green Bottles* on the bus and *The front of the bus they canni sing*.   Everyone racing about in the sun.   Away from the town.   The blackboard.   I thought it was cool to sweat but I felt I wasn't sweating enough so I licked my fingers and rubbed them on my forehead.   That's better.   I'm running down by a river. A loud cold wild torrent.   It would be easy to slip and fall. My body swallowed away in the froth.   I didn't imagine it. Mrs. Brady's voice bellowing from the bridge.   *FULTON!*

I bought a plastic deer in a souvenir shop for mum.   I bought a small ceramic dog made in the USSR.   A gift from very far away.   I'd saved my pocket money.   It made me feel grown-up.   Able to think on my own.

Gordon wrote on the wall of the school BRADY GO HOME. Mrs. Brady. Dark haired. Scary. Good at her job. Got results. Dad found out. Marched him round and made him clean it off. It was only chalk. Easily removed. Before anyone found out. Nobody found out. Only we knew. Brady didn't go home.

In the school bushes in the school holiday. Down by the fence. Boys and girls sitting talking. Laughing. Blowing away the dandelion clocks. Sticking buttercups under our chins. Laughing about silly things that make their own sense. Listening to the radio. Someone singing about loving a flower girl. Someone singing about an Underworld. Someone singing about not letting Maggie go. Someone singing about seeing for miles and miles. A hot slow world. Happy together.

Do Not Adjust Your Set. Time Tunnel. Danger Man. Bewitched. Combat. Batman. Jimmy Clitheroe. Voyage to the Bottom of the Sea. Tarzan. Banana Splits. The Monkees. Quick Before They Catch Us Everybody Run. Harry Worth. Steptoe and Son. Till Death Us Do Part. Hogan's Heroes. Land of the Giants. Robinson Crusoe. The theme music from Robinson Crusoe. The Flashing Blade. The Virginian. Mission Impossible. Wacky Races. Scooby-Doo. Z Cars. The Fugitive. Tom Grattan's War. Adam Adamant. The Saint. Please Sir! Man in a Suitcase. The Champions. The Prisoner. Simon Dee. Big Breadwinner Hog. Monty Python's Flying Circus. No VHS, no DVD, no download, no upload, no endless repeats. One shot. The Singing Ringing Tree. The evil laughing dwarf looking down from a cloud. The evil laughing dwarf hiding inside a rock and shaking his fist. The evil laughing dwarf flying in circles. A big fish gulping for air. Star Trek, for the first time.

The opening titles of The Great War. A camera sinking down through a black and white trench and stopping suddenly at the skeleton of a soldier still in uniform. His arm at a strange angle. Edging slowly to the left with epic melancholy music and finally painfully slowly moving in on the haunted face of a Tommy as he stares out at us and the name of the latest episode appears on the screen. A million miles from childhood games. Brutal innocence.

Sun. Again. We'd skip down to the shop and buy round red lollipops in bags of white sherbet and floppy black cords of liquorice in yellow papery tubes and packs of love hearts with stuff like kiss me quick written on them and swizels which were like smaller versions of love hearts only without the writing and lucky bags full of things you couldn't see which was part of the thrill and more red lollipops in see-through wrappers and chunky green and pink lollipops on thin sticks and Bazooka Joe bubble gum and little tins of soapy water and a ring to blow bubbles with and real glass bottles of dark cola or limeade and comics with heroes who could do anything inside them and pop comics with pictures of Amen Corner and Manfred Mann and The Herd and Long John Baldry and The Beach Boys and The Who and The Kinks and Procul Harum and The Byrds and The Animals and The Troggs and The Zombies and The Hollies and The Beatles and The Archies who weren't real inside them and rolls of caps with tiny black spots on light green paper which smelled of gunpowder when you put them into your gun and aimed at the nearest girl and fired and plastic water pistols coloured red or blue or green which squirted thin jets of cold water from the tap into our red excited faces or open mouths if it was incredibly hot for weeks and weeks which it always was.

There must have been some rainy days.   It's easy not to remember.

In Craig Morrison's garage doing our own version of Zabadak by Dave Dee, Dozy, Beaky, Mick and Tich. Me drumming on a lawnmower bin. Craig twanging a toy Huckleberry Hound guitar. Steven doing something else. All of us singing. Zabadak Zabadak. Kara Ka Kora Ka Karakak. Something like that. A garage band. Hoping no one can hear us.

Craig Morrison had more than me. A black poodle called Bimbo. A scary mum who looked like a witch. The Johnny Seven One-Man-Army. Grenades. Rocket launcher. Small Batman and Robin figures. Pristine Batmobile. James Bond Aston Martin with ejector seat. The latest Action Man with fuzzy hair. An armoured car. Out of my league. A silver plane from a cereal box. A free gift. I wanted it. He left it in the frogspawn burn on the primary school waste ground. Glittering beneath the surface. He wouldn't miss it. It was nothing. I dipped my hand and took it and ran home. I had to give it back. A shiny small black gondola he left in the weeds at the side of his garage. I took it and ran home. He was told not to play with me ever again. I am a thief. I did it. It was me.

Up to the top of Atholl Crescent to pick brambles. Stuff them into bags for our mums to make jam. Then up Honeybog Hill to the radar of the old Renfrew airport. Round. White. Derelict. Dark glassless windows. The ground covered with rubble. Like the world had ended recently and still had a memory of itself. The view down to the railway line and the old runway where the new motorway is going to be. Then into the tower and up the ladder to the first floor. Clang the trapdoor behind us. It felt dangerous. Separate. We'd kick stuff around. Light a fire like a song by The Doors. Return.

Guns of Navarone. Bridge on the River Kwai. The Magnificent Seven. Zulu. Goldfinger. A Hard Day's Night. Chitty Chitty Bang Bang. Born Free. How the West Was Won. The Sand Pebbles. One Million Years BC. Carry On Cleo. Carry On Spying. Half a Sixpence. Ben Hur. Planet of the Apes. Mary Poppins. Snow White and the Seven Dwarfs. The Wizard of Oz. One of Our Spies is Missing. Munster, Go Home! Zulu. True Grit. A Man Called Flintstone. In Search of the Castaways. Blackbeard's Ghost. Batman. Zulu. Where Eagles Dare. Cheyenne Autumn. Carry On Up the Khyber. The Love Bug. Our Man Flint. Doctor Who and the Daleks. Thunderbirds are Go. The Sound of Music. Mackenna's Gold. You Only Live Twice. Spartacus. On Her Majesty's Secret Service. The Alamo. The Green Berets. Is Paris Burning? Robinson Crusoe on Mars. Butch Cassidy and the Sundance Kid. Carry On Camping. Zulu. Kes. Some of these were re-releases. I was too young for Shalako but Gordon told me how the Indians made a woman eat her own diamonds. Superb. I didn't get into Bonnie and Clyde.

An unofficial hierarchy. Travelling from east to west. The Kelburne was the best cinema. Classy. The La Scala was in the middle. Nice. The ABC was the fleapit. Tatty. Sometimes The Mosspark for a double bill of Zulu and Robinson Crusoe on Mars. Sometimes The Coliseum in Glasgow for something posh. No multiplexes. One cinema one screen. Double features. You could stay all day if you wanted to. Round and round. Sitting up the back eating Aztec bars and saying *Aztec!* in dramatic gravelly voices while watching Pathé News and Pearl and Dean. Ba-ba Ba-ba Ba-ba Ba-ba Ba-ba-ba. Squinting out into the light.

In the sweet shop next to The Kelburne I asked for a Ripple. I was too quiet. *Sorry son, what was that?* Can I have a Ripple please. Still too quiet. *Sorry son?* CAN I HAVE A RIPPLE PLEASE! said in a tone brimming with embarrassment and fury. Dad killing himself laughing.

The Boys' Brigade Sportagama. The Big Show. In the afternoon we went for a walk past Third Lanark's football ground. Weedy stone terraces. Like something from a dead civilisation. We waited our turn in a school classroom while watching Scotland play Wales on the television. 5-3 to us. Then out and down and onto the stage. Jumping. Leaping. Whistling. Doing things I never wanted to do again.

Marching up and down. Marching diagonally. Making nice patterns. Wearing a sailor's cap and dark blue shorts. Saluting the flag and singing songs about anchors. Miss Rinn was nice. I got three merit badges on one night. I learnt to play the recorder and cover the holes in the right order. Do the right thing. I'd had enough. I left them behind. They came to our door to find out why. A tall thin man and a wee fat man. I stayed in bed. Dad told them it wasn't for me. I could hear them talking but kept quiet. Holding my breath. They went away but said they'd come back. They didn't. They gave up on me.

I broke a window and I ran away. I'd been throwing stones at my friend and it all went wrong. The glass on their front door cracked. I ran home and went into the lounge and climbed onto the window sill behind the curtains with my back to the window. I suppose I thought I could stay there till the end of time. They could see me from the outside. Not too smart. Mum and dad had to pay.

Lights out. Late. The TV flickering. Mum and dad in the Hanna's next door. Jimmy would come in and we'd watch Don't Watch Alone. The old black and white horror films. Dracula. Frankenstein. The Mummy. Various family members. Sons, brides, daughters. Someone would check we were okay from time to time. The sound of music through the wall. I'd fall asleep and miss the end. The credits would be rolling when I woke. The following week the roles would be reversed and we'd go next door. The sound of music through the wall. Jimmy had a better TV. The Fall of the House of Usher in shocking colour. Dad would come in and say *What News from the Holy Land!* Jimmy had a model of The Wolfman on his bedside table with the hands glued on the wrong way round. I kept a list of all the horror films I'd seen. Tick the names of the different stars. Karloff. Lugosi. Frye. Atwill. Chaney Junior. Lorre. Price. The monsters under control.

Mum in the back garden. Hanging out the washing. The wind blowing. Shirts. Underpants. Towels. Sheets. Moving slowly along and attaching things to the lines. It gets harder to see her as the lines are filled. The sheets flapping. Obscuring the view. I'll go out later and pick up the dropped pegs.

Mum told us about a young girl she once worked with called Monica. Long before we were born. Mum had a watch stolen and Monica was very sympathetic and said how terrible it was and mum said she knew in a flash that it was Monica who had stolen it and the police came in and investigated and they found the watch in her drawer. There it was. That was that. Mum knew. She just knew. She'll never forget the feeling.

When the Star Trek theme tune began dad would make a whooshing sound at particular points and would stretch out his arm like he was reaching towards the end of the universe. We'd encourage him and then after a while we'd say *Stop it dad, that's rubbish.* He'd also say things like RAKA-TAKA-TAKA-TAKA TAK-TAK TAK and *Bring me my Phial!* for no apparent reason which is the best reason of all.

Dad's inhaler for his bronchitis. His wheeze. A loud whirring frightening contraption he'd put in his mouth and suck. We'd watch in silence. In horror.

Hanging from the monkey bars in the school playground. Playing kiss kick cuddle and torture at the garages. A small round lamp on the floor of one that looked like a tiny UFO. We stared through the window. Pretended to be scared. Playing on the American swings down at Allanton. Playing headers and wally and keepie-up and three 'n' in. Pulling crab apples from the tree. Pullying itchycoos from the bushes and popping them apart. Little seeds. Lying in a bedsheet tent with Anne Linn in her wee blue swimsuit in her back garden. The sun filtering through the cotton. Sitting on top of the school shed looking at a picture of a lady showing her breasts and wearing black stockings. Something new. Something we should know about.

The Tyrannosaurus Rex at Kelvingrove. Standing proud. Staring down. Fierce teeth and beady eyes. Like the one from One Million Years BC. I liked to draw the creatures from the film. The Allosaurus. The big turtle. The scary apemen in the cave. Raquel Welch in a fur bikini. Somehow exciting. Gordon had a poster of her on the bedroom wall. Larger than life. The beginning of time. A Pterodactyl suspended from the ceiling.

I woke, went into mum and dad's bedroom. Some reason. A glass of water. Mum and dad were under the sheets. The sheets were moving. Something I shouldn't see. They didn't hear. I turned and went out and closed the door, but not completely. They never knew. I found the water myself.

Looking for something.   Pulling open the top drawer of
mum and dad's chest of drawers and finding a comic called
WEIRD.   A picture of a vampire and a werewolf fighting on
the cover.   I knew it was a Christmas present for me.   I didn't
touch it.   I looked at the colours.   Dark green.   Red.   The
word *WEIRD* written in a horrific shivery blood-drippy kind
of way.   It hadn't been hidden.   I shouldn't have been there.
I closed the drawer.   I looked at it 3 or 4 more times over the
next few weeks.   I didn't touch it.   One day I opened the
drawer and it was gone.   I got it that Christmas along with
another comic which must have been underneath it all the
time and whose name I can't remember.

Saturday afternoon in Glasgow.   Late December and
getting dark.   Mad traffic.   Christmas lights.   Looking in
Tam Shepherd's Trick Shop at fake dog turds and stink
bombs.   We go to see Santa in his grotto.   Say what we want
for Christmas.   I think I still wanted to believe but knew
it was really mum and dad.   Fair enough.   A sign outside
a newsagent says THE WORLD WAITS FOR APOLLO
8.   Pictures of Earth from far away.   A tiny child's marble
hanging in black.   Lonely.   I asked for a spacesuit.

Charging downstairs in our pyjamas and into the lounge and there are two huge white pillowcases on the couch. One for Gordon and one for me. Stuffed with Christmas stuff. We stand and stare. Almost too good to touch. Captain Scarlet. Johnny West. A brown plastic castle and knights to go with it. An Action Man astronaut suit. Silver with a zip. Annuals from gran that were signed by dad. Selection boxes. Chocolate covered coins in little nets hanging from the tree. Chocolate humans wrapped in foil. A smiling snowman made out of the same thing they make egg boxes out of. A tiny plastic Nativity scene in the same place every year. Fallen green needles on the carpet. Still dark outside. Mum got a fur coat.

Stanley Baxter dressed as a woman at the King's Theatre. Parliamo Glasgow.   Francie and Josie in a Christmas Pantomime. Bob's Your Uncle the creepy community hall magician. Puppets and singsongs. The circus at the Kelvin Hall with big fat Jen. Clowns with collapsing cars. Dogs in Rangers and Celtic strips playing football. A pyramid of police motorcyclists in Bellahouston Park. A wacky clown policeman bringing comic relief in between the main events. Cycling about and falling over. We selected him for special treatment. Whenever he came near we laughed loudly in an obvious over the top way to emphasise that he wasn't funny at all.   It went on for ages.   Cruel.   Whenever he came round. I could see in his eyes that he wanted to kill us.

Down the Clyde on the Waverley.   Past the shipyards on the north bank. The QE2 in its dock. Almost ready to be launched. Majestic. Huge. Proud. The sound of hammers and metal and machines and rivets being banged in place. Fire and brimstone. A buzzing hive. The workers waving as we paddle past. Getting smaller. Gone.

The school camp at Aberfoyle. Butterflies. Nature. Watching a rubbishy film called Bonnie Prince Charlie screened on a rubbishy projector. Watching Anne Linn and Laura Downs singing White Horses at the rubbishy concert.   Sleeping in a long bunk bed dormitory and running to get my vitamin C. Burnt porridge. Standing in the corner for being bad during the breakfast rammy. A few of us. Heads bowed beside a large silver shiny round tin with jam at the bottom. Smeared to the sides. A trap for the wasps. They were all stuck in it. Fizzing. Furious. Moving but going nowhere. Becoming still. The place wasps come to die.

Practising for weeks for the school concert. The boys had to do somersaults and tumble about on rubber mats and demonstrate exercises. I was always out of synchronisation with the others. My arms were coming down as theirs were going up. My legs were going out as theirs were coming in. My brain was telling me the wrong thing. We worked on it and got it right. It was going to be fine. On the night of the concert I was completely wrong. My legs were going out as theirs were coming in. My arms were coming down as theirs were going up. It was the rest that was wrong. Not me. Surely. I could see the audience smiling. I could see the teacher glaring and snarling my name. *FULTON!*

The girls on stage dancing to Albatross. Grass skirts made of paper. Rhythmically moving their hips and their arms. The boys silent. Songs about ice cream and nice girls who love sailors. I painted the large ice cream cones on the scenery but wasn't allowed anywhere near the stage.

We were given pen pals to write to. Dowanhill primary school. I got a girl. I sent a couple of letters and got two in return. Words and pictures. It was nice. Then I didn't write any more. I don't know why. Everyone else kept on going. I got letters asking me why I'm not writing. Becoming more angry. I didn't reply. One day we were taken to an event at the Kelvin Hall so we could meet our pen pals. Nightmare. Once inside I spent the whole day dodging and hiding. Moving from one place to another. Losing myself in the crowd. Someone came up and asked me if I was Graham Fulton. Maybe it was her. I said no. She might kill me. On the way home on the bus one of my classmates said they just wanted to talk to me and didn't mind if I didn't want to write any more. They just wanted to know why. I don't know why. I have nothing to tell them.

5th prize for Scottish Literature.   Reading a poem out loud.
I chose a book called The Black Octopus.   I went up on
stage and collected it at the prize giving at the end of the
year. Red tie. White shirt. Grey shorts. Next thing I knew
they were calling my name again to come up and collect
my first prize for Art.   Everyone clapping.   Smiling.   The
light streaming through the windows.   A book called King
Solomon's Mines. Mine.

On the carpet in front of the telly.   Women playing tennis.
Mum ironing.   Clothes drying on the clothes horse.   Mum
says if she wins this next point then she's the champion. She
does. Anne Hayden Jones from Britain. Really ugly.

Mum singing a song about a baby going down a plughole.
Now your baby's happy, she ain't gonna weep no more. Words of
wisdom. Words that know the way of the world.

Mum disguised the mince in a pie. I ate it. Grew up all right.
Taller than Ronnie Corbett. Smaller than Boris Karloff.

Things in the toy cupboard.   Overflowing shelves. Thunderbirds models except for Thunderbird 5.   A panda with pulled-out eyes.   A Thunderbirds uniform.   A Thunderbirds gun. Supercar. A teddy bear. A spinning top. A wooden canoe. A stagecoach. A globe. A monkey with cymbals. Batman badges. Happy Smile Club badges. Spectrum badges.   Golden Shred Golliwog badges.   A gyroscope.   A kaleidoscope.   A microscope.   History of Flight coins. Army helmets. A US Cavalry hat. An Indian chief's headdress with the red feathers falling out. Tim Goes to Sea book.   Five Find-Outer books.   Torchy the Battery Boy Annuals.   Rupert the Bear Annuals.   Jack and Jill comics with Walter Hottle Bottle. I-Spy books partly filled-in.   Ladybird books about bibles and trains.   A Churchill funeral commemorative coin. A pictorial history of Britain ending with the First World War. Biggles books. Tales from the Arabian Knights. Robin Annuals. Stingray Annuals. Doctor Who Annuals. Victor Annuals. Hotspur Annuals. Valiant Annuals. Books about animals. Books about birds. Cat in the Hat. Piles of Look and Learns. The Trigan Empire. A Spanish galleon jigsaw puzzle.   First Encyclopedia in Colour. Smiling children from other countries dancing in a circle. Model planes and tubes of glue. A little box of paints. Transfers for the back of the hand. The Broons. Oor Wullie. Black Bob the Dandy Wonder Dog. Books about dinosaurs. Books about lost cities. Books about war. Famous Monsters of Filmland magazines. Piles of drawings. Matchbox cars. Dinky cars. Marbles in a jar. Snow White building blocks. Lego. Ludo. Lot's Bricks. Snakes and Ladders. Subbuteo. Cluedo. Monopoly. Blow football. Draughts. Dominoes. A fort. Battle of the Little Big Horn. D-Day Landings in convincing plastic. Flotsam and jetsam. All crammed in. The 60s. Creaking behind the closed doors.

Dad getting some books out and putting some back in. The little ticket in its sleeve. Walking the shelves on Saturday morning. The unique smell of the Stirling Library in Glasgow. The smell of ideas. The smell of no one talking. The sound of slow footsteps. Dad got me The Iron Man by someone called Ted Hughes. I sat at the table and looked as he continued searching the alcoves. I liked the pictures. Poetic cartoons.

Watching Celtic win the European Cup in black and white. Watching Manchester United win the European Cup in black and white. George Best going round the goalkeeper. Watching Scotland lose 4-1 at Wembley in black and white. Watching Scotland lose 3-2 to West Germany in West Germany in black and white. Sitting on the wall at Ibrox watching Rangers play Newcastle in real life in colour with thousands and thousands of people and the green grass and the deafening noise and men pissing into beer cans and pouring it down the steps. There's no memory of England winning the World Cup.

Watching Manchester City play Everton in Manchester. Mum's sister lived there. Sky blue shirts. Green grass. Everyone packed in. We got in late and missed the first goal. The Everton fans chanting EVERTON. The City fans replying SHIT.

Apollo 11 on the launch pad.   A white smoking missile on the other side of the world. Voices. Bright sun. Something incredible. Really happening. Armstrong saying everything feels good. *What if it goes wrong? What if it crashes?* Thought but not said out loud.   The countdown going from minutes to seconds. Our living room. Armstrong. Aldrin. Collins. Exciting. Frightening. *Zero. Lift off. We have a lift off. 32 minutes past the hour.* Watching until it becomes a dot. Until the dot burns into nothing. Go out to play.

The middle of the night at Ardfern. Somewhere between the dark and the dawn. Listening to men walk on the moon on the radio. No television in the cottage. Wanting to sleep. Not wanting to sleep. Looking with wonder at the transistor. Looking out of the window to try and see the moon. See the men walking. The insect spacecraft. Sleeping. Reading the papers in the Culfail Hotel on the following day. Black and white pictures of three men with short hair. Not flower people. The word TACITURN next to the picture of Michael Collins staring out of the page at me. I didn't know what it meant. The beautiful moon. Touched for the first time. Lost.

Mum and dad went off to the Galley of Lorne for a drink. We went out and walked along the road that runs along the side of the loch and found a good spot and lay down on the road and pretended to be dead. Pretended we'd been knocked over. What a laugh. The first car screeched to a halt. We got up and ran down and hid in the rocks. Keeping really quiet. The car moved on. We'd gotten away with it. Yes. He recognised us of course and told mum and dad. We hadn't thought of that.

The jetty near Craignish Point. We'd scrabble about for a while then walk as far as we could in the direction of the end of land. Gordon nearly went over an edge until dad called for him to stop. Dad took our pictures standing at what we thought was a fort then took our pictures pretending to be clinging to the top of a cliff. As if we were about to fall. The whirlpool in the background between Scarba and Jura. The Sound calm. Nothing what it looks to be.

Gordon caught a Mackerel off the jetty. A lovely silver fish with cobalt markings. He had his picture taken with it. I had my picture taken as well so I didn't feel left out. Mum gutted it with her nose screwed up in disgust. When she wasn't looking a cat came in the window and carried it off. Oh how she laughed.

Me, Gordon, Jimmy, Des, Graham, Alan. Our own Olympics. One lap of the block. 2 laps of the block. 5 laps of the block. On our bikes around the block. Sprints on the road when no cars are coming. Sweat dripping. Hearts banging. The same boy always last. Alan. Only ourselves to beat.

We formed Atholl Crescent Dynamo and we played other teams at football. We recruited players from other streets. Dougie Gregor. Enzo Durante who sounded exotic. We tried to dress in white. The easiest colour to co-ordinate. Moreville beat us 9-3 on a sunny Saturday morning. The pitch seemed huge. I went on a spectacular run down the right wing. Dodging tackles. We beat them 9-4 on another Saturday night. I scored an own goal and the other team sniggered. Jimmy Hanna scored with the last kick of the game from the halfway line against Ralston Rapide. We grabbed the ball and ran away. All over. I kept the scores and the scorers and the dates in a small handmade stapled pad. Dad's old army crest was the club badge. It was thrown out later on when I didn't seem to care.

We'd march down to the primary school grass to play football singing *Fight the good fight!* to some tune of our own creation. A man would set his evil black dog Tanya on us which we later renamed MATONGO. He didn't like kids playing football too close to his garden. We'd climb the palings and Tanya would be down below us snarling and foaming and trying to rip our throats out. She never did. The dog of death.

We played football on the waste ground with the boys from Penilee. A no man's land between different worlds. George was one of them. We played a bit and had a laugh. We went to meet him one day but saw him being carried away by people with dark blood coming out of his head and streaming down his face and neck. He'd been bashed with a half brick from a building site. He didn't see me watching. I never saw him again.

A classroom concert. Some of us picked to perform. I was going to do my impressions. Steptoe and Son. I'd done them many times before. Knew them back to front. Everyone loved them. I screwed my face up really well. This time I got it wrong and said *You dirty old man* in Albert's voice instead of Harold's. The right words in the wrong voice. The only time. Everyone loved it anyway. Mrs. Brady smiled. She knew what I was talking about.

Apollo 12. Men on the Moon for the second time. Conrad and Bean. Everyone in the school hall watching an empty television screen. Expectant. Mesmerised. Cross-legged on the floor. The astronauts' camera was broken. Accents and beeps from beyond the sky. No surface. No helmets. The deep black expanse of space. It made it more real.

Mrs. Brady realised I couldn't see the blackboard and moved me to the front. Everything was fine. I could even do the sums.

Dad listening to his barrelhouse organ jazz LP and having a wee whisky. A serious lapse in taste. We'd wait patiently as if we weren't listening then quickly spin round and loudly mimic the annoying twiddly bit of organ that happened at the end of every song and do the finger movements as well. Every single song. As each one came to its end we'd expertly pretend we'd forgotten all about it and weren't really bothered then suddenly do it again. Ha Ha. Eventually dad stormed out and got into his car and reversed up the drive, only stopping momentarily to wind down his window and give us a huge V-sign as we looked out the lounge window at him with the two of us and mum all laughing.

Hogmanay. Shortbread. Gran's ginger wine. We'd go round the houses. The adults shaking hands and kissing and carrying whisky and lumps of coal. They'd get drunk. Sing and dance. Mr. Mason wobbling about. *I am the rubber man.* We'd eat cheese footballs and slices of pineapple and cheese on a stick. Mr. McLellan liked to squeeze our hands hard to show how strong he was. A grown man. Watch our expressions as he tightened harder. Welcome to the world of adults. In our beds when we tried to go to sleep our eyes stung from the cigarette smoke. The smoke of the decade. 69 into 70.

Things I have no memory of but I know happened. People told me. I saw photographs. Gordon washed my face with a dirty dish cloth as I sat in my pram quite happily letting him do it. I filled an empty can of Tennent's lager with grotty water from the primary school burn and drank it along with parts of a dead frog. Gordon came out of school and walked all the way to gran's house without telling anyone. Gordon ran away from home and hid at the top of the Crescent. We lived in Dunchurch Road for a short while before moving into number 55. We lived in Benedict Drive in London before coming to Scotland. Near Heathrow. We'd go and look at the planes landing. I'd run into our next door neighbour's house and straight up the stairs to get Keith's cowboy hat from under his bed and come back down screwing it round and round on my head so it wouldn't fall off. I fell asleep with my cheeks full of food I didn't want to swallow. I was born. I was in mum's inside. I was nowhere.

The Shrinking Man(Richard Mathieson)
~~Fahrenheit 451(Ray Bradbury)~~
~~Mysterious Island(Jules Verne)~~ Nisrq.l.b
From the Earth to the Moon(Jules Verne)
Off on a Comet(Jules Verne)
~~The Island of Doctor Moreau(H.G Wells)~~
~~Fantastic Voyage(Isaac Asimov)~~
Dark eyes of London(Edgar Wallace)
Frankenstein(Mary Shelley)
~~Psycho(Robert Bloch)~~
~~I,Robot(Isaac Asimov)~~

Reading real books. For fun. Treasure Island. Journey to the Centre of the Earth. The Invisible Man. Edgar Allan Poe. I used dad's typewriter and carefully typed on a piece of paper all of the books I'd like to read and gave it to dad. He bought as many as he could in the time allowed and put a blue line through each one bought. I would get one at Christmas. Birthday. Others here and there. No particular occasion necessary. The occasion of being alive.

Files within files. The images that never go. Good. Bad. Bewildering. Clear. The moments themselves are pure. It's the harvesting that squeezes the heart. A state of mind to be reclaimed.

There's always been a small brass musical box all the way from Chile. A grey key to wind it up. A tiny haunting tune going round and round. I don't know its name. The mechanism inside full of things moving and turning. A comb-like structure plucking the raised notes on a lazily turning barrel. Slowly slowing down until it comes to a stop. Stop. Comes to the end. The last note hanging in the thin air.

We're on a train journey and I'm very young. A station with a glass canopy. No one about. Trees. Quiet. Not in a city. Mum and Gordon, but not dad. We must be going ahead and he'll be following later on. That has to be it. Going to live in Scotland. A fragile early memory. So faint it's almost not there. Elusive. Happy. Green trees. The roof above our heads. Where is it? What was happening? No one here to ask.

A sad tram on a cold dark misty night. Sparks and a crowd watching it go. Maybe the final one. Maybe a dream that was never even there. An end of something. A start of something else.

I often think of those days.   Of the summers and winters.
Suns and moons.   Of Jimmy and Des, of Jimmy and May,
of Doreen and Jeraldine, of Jerry and Mauraide, of Ron and
Craig, of Mrs. Brady and Mr. Begg, of Alan and Anne, of
Gran and Gran.   Of Gordon, and Fergus, and Jessie.   Of
those named and those unnamed.   Those remembered and
not forgotten.

The Man is Son of the Child.

Lightning Source UK Ltd.
Milton Keynes UK
UKOW03f1540060813

214936UK00004B/26/P